FASTBACK® *Spy*

Dangerous Waters

KEN GIRARD

GLOBE FEARON
Pearson Learning Group

FASTBACK® SPY BOOKS

The Cobra
Dangerous Waters
Double Exposure
Flight of the Sparrow
The Ham Who Cried Wolf

The Last Hand
The Legend
Pension Plan
The Search for El Cuchillo
The Trap

Cover Stockbyte. All photography © Pearson Education, Inc. (PEI) unless specifically noted.

Copyright © 2004 by Pearson Education, Inc., publishing as Globe Fearon®, an imprint of Pearson Learning Group, 299 Jefferson Road, Parsippany, NJ 07054. All rights reserved. No part of this book may be reproduced or transmitted in any form or by any means, electronic or mechanical, including photocopying, recording, or by any information storage and retrieval system, without permission in writing from the publisher. For information regarding permission(s), write to Rights and Permissions Department.

Globe Fearon® and Fastback® are registered trademarks of Globe Fearon, Inc.

ISBN 0-13-024611-5
Printed in the United States of America
1 2 3 4 5 6 7 8 9 10   07 06 05 04 03

1-800-321-3106
www.pearsonlearning.com

The night fog swirled around the small coastal town of Wallingford. The low moan of the foghorn cut through the thick blanket of air rushing inland from the Pacific Ocean. Dave Colvin sat on the edge of the wooden pier, his hands jammed into the pockets of a Navy jacket, and stared into the darkness.

Everything had gone wrong since he had met John Bradley. What was supposed to be a simple job had turned into a hard case. Bradley had called him in San Diego and said, "Dave, I want you to come up to Wallingford. It's a simple dive. All you have to do is work on some cables."

"Some simple dive," Colvin muttered.

A job which should have taken 2 weeks had dragged into a month. "Hang in there," Bradley had said. But Dave had become disgusted. Finally, he had asked to be paid off. Bradley agreed to pay him the next morning. But he never showed up. Instead, Dave learned, he had packed his gear and run out.

So now, Dave Colvin sat on the Wallingford dock. He was alone in a strange seaport, and almost broke.

A blast of cool, wet air followed him as he trudged from the dock over to the waterfront section of town. It was a tough neighborhood.

Dave kept an eye out for trouble as he walked past the neon lights and headed toward "The Rusty Pelican." It was a diner he'd been eating at regularly.

"Back again?" Barney Phillips asked, as Dave came ambling through the door. Barney, a stocky man with a scar on his face, owned the diner. He shoved a mug of coffee into Dave's hand. "I heard John Bradley took off without finishing his contract."

"Or paying me," Dave replied.

"That figures," Barney said. "I knew he was a deadbeat from the moment he came swaggering into this place."

Barney leaned across the counter. "How would you like to make some *real* money?"

"I just want to scrape enough together to go back to San Diego. And then I want to forget this whole thing."

Barney leaned closer and whispered,

"Listen, my friend, a man with your talents should be swimming in dough, not the muck in Wallingford Channel. There's a guy who's been in here looking for very experienced divers."

Dave laughed. "Up here? Why? Aren't there enough local skin divers to hunt lobsters?"

"He's not local and he's hunting *treasure*."

"C'mon, Barney, that's ridiculous."

Barney Phillips set his jaw and looked Dave straight in the eye. "Have you seen the *Global Explorer* anchored outside the breakwater?"

"The large merchant ship?"

"That's the one. Big enough for you, my friend? The man comes into Wallingford from that vessel. I heard he's got a crew of fifty aboard. The word is, now he's scouting for a crack underwater man who's had experience with salvage."

Dave sipped his coffee. "A treasure hunter? What's he looking for?"

"I don't know," Barney whispered. "Rumor has it he's going to the China Sea this week."

"When does he come in?" Dave asked.

Barney pounded him on the shoulder and smiled. "That's the way to talk. Stick around. He'll be back in a day or two."

Three more days went by, but the man from the *Global Explorer* didn't appear. "It's not going to work out," Dave grumbled. "I'm going to hitch-hike back down south."

"Patience, Davey," Barney said as he poured him a cup of coffee. Just then the door opened and Barney looked up. "What did I tell you, Davey. He's here."

They looked across the diner. A tall, well-built man with sharp features walked towards them. "I hear you found a diver we could use aboard the *Explorer*," he said to Barney.

"You're standing next to him, mister," Barney replied. "Dave Colvin, this is, er . . ."

"Nick Frush." The man smiled slightly at Dave as they shook hands. "I'm the captain and owner of the *Global Explorer*."

Dave and Frush moved to a small booth

and began to talk at length about diving, shark attacks, and the newest equipment.

"It seems you're qualified," Frush said, "but I'd like to see you in the water. Come out to the ship tomorrow, and if everything goes well I'll sign you up."

"See, my boy," Barney said after Frush had left, "your luck's changing."

"Really?" Dave shook his head. "We talked about everything *except* where they were going, what he was hunting, and how much I would be paid. He's a strange one, Barney, and I don't know if I trust him. I've been burned once before—by Bradley."

"What have you got to lose, Davey?" Barney said. "You're broke and you've got no other prospects."

"I guess you're right," he said.

A silver speedboat met Dave at the pier the next morning. It churned through the calm waters and sped towards the *Global Explorer* anchored off the coast.

Captain Frush greeted Dave as the speedboat pulled alongside. "Welcome aboard. Ready for a tour?"

"Yes, sir," Dave replied as he climbed up the ship's ladder.

"Come with me. I want you to see this new piece of equipment."

Dave followed him down a hatch into the depths of the vessel. As they walked through the compartments Dave saw stacks of neatly stored diving gear, boxes of welding tools, and all the supplies needed for underwater work.

"Here it is," Frush announced as he opened a metal door. Dave was stunned. In the center of this huge compartment was a small diving submarine. "She's the only one like it in the world, Dave."

Dave was speechless. It wasn't only the minisub that amazed him. It was the other pieces of equipment laid out on the floor as well. There were several high-speed underwater sleds and stacks of harpoon guns. Next to them was a small underwater tractor, more welding tools, and rows of diving suits.

"Where did you get all this equipment?" Dave asked. He examined an odd-looking wet suit.

"Let's just say a rich uncle," Frush replied. "Oh, that suit is the most up-to-date kind that money can buy. You can dive one, two thousand feet without feeling the pressure. And all the gear is the best."

The two men climbed into the submarine. Dave was very impressed. The safety systems, the controls, and the photographic supplies were quite advanced. "What's this?" he asked, pointing to a control box.

"Underwater protection. The sub is armed with five laser guns. Just to beat away sharks," Frush added quickly. "You can't trust those creatures, can you?"

"No," Dave answered softly. "But laser guns? Why such powerful . . . ?"

"Why don't we get into some of those new wet suits and take a quick dive?" Frush interrupted. "I'll check you out on the gear and see what you can do underwater."

Dave agreed. Frush handed him a new wet suit and picked one out for himself. They dressed in silence and then went topside. Dave was first in the water, then Frush. They dove one hundred, then two hundred feet onto the sloping floor of the waters just off the coast. Dave swam easily through the water. He thought the equipment was the lightest and best he had ever worn.

A mass of small fish surrounded him as he and Frush rose to the surface. "You handle yourself quite well," Frush remarked as they headed back to the ship. "Did you ever do any underwater welding and demolition?"

Dave said that he had and described his

work with torches, pipe construction, and repairs.

"Well, all of this looks and sounds good," Frush decided. "I have a simple deal for you. We pay a flat fee for the voyage. In your case it'll be $25,000."

Dave whistled softly.

"I'll put half in a bank account for you before we ship out, and give you the other half when we return to port. It's straight underwater salvaging and digging. We provide all the gear."

"Very fair," Dave replied. He thought for a moment and then asked, "Where are we heading? And what are you looking for?"

Frush smiled. "We're going to a spot off the China coast. I'm after a Spanish treasure ship that sank in 1745."

"That sounds exciting. Well, I'd like to join the crew. A sunken treasure ship? It beats staying in Wallingford."

Frush smiled. The men shook hands. "Welcome aboard, Dave."

That evening, Dave leaned against the rail of the ship as it plowed through the dark water. He felt good. Captain Frush was true to his word: $12,500 was deposited in Dave's name in the Wallingford Savings Bank. The contract he signed said the remaining sum was due "upon return."

The ship picked up speed, and the wind blew softly across the bow. The stars shone brightly in the early evening sky. He was headed for sunken treasure. Yes, his luck certainly had changed.

The next morning Captain Frush showed Dave a series of charts. They were maps of the area in which the "treasure" was thought to be. Dave examined the details of the water's depth—nearly a thousand feet—and the currents. It wasn't going to be an easy dive. The rock formations under the water seemed jagged and dangerous. Dave studied the charts and considered the plan of attack.

The *Global Explorer* headed south, then north, then west. Dave noticed these changes in the course. But he was too interested in his work to question the constant changes in the route. Each day he talked with Frush, then checked the submarine and the other equipment.

The days wore on and Dave noticed that the ship was changing course every 12 hours. They should have been nearing the dive area, but they were still far from it. He began to feel uneasy. Perhaps Frush had lied to him.

On the morning of their tenth day at sea Dave was on the bridge with Captain Frush again. "Here's another set of charts," Frush said quietly and handed Dave a computer printout. "I think that the starboard bow will be the best point of entry to the ship, don't you?"

Dave was about to answer when a siren squawked loudly. Then a voice came over the PA system, "UNIDENTIFIED CRAFT THREE MILES TO PORT BOW. TAKE STATIONS. TAKE STATIONS." Dave looked down at the deck. It was filled with men running to large crates at the bow and stern.

"What's going on?" Dave shouted.

"Just stay here and you won't get hurt," Frush cautioned.

The men pulled the sides of the crates to the deck revealing two large guns.

"All hands to battle stations," Frush shouted into a microphone.

"TWO MILES AND CLOSING," the PA blared.

"One-seventy to starboard. Cut speed," Frush told the helmsman.

"STAND DOWN. STAND DOWN," the

PA voice said. "VESSEL IDENTIFIED. MERCHANT SHIP OFF COURSE. ALL HANDS RETURN TO NORMAL DUTIES. STOW ALL WEAPONS."

Capt. Frush breathed a sigh of relief. He glanced at Dave and smiled slightly. "Well, that was a close one. I guess you're wondering what . . ."

"I certainly am," Dave shot back. "What is going on? And what are we after?"

"You're aboard a very special ship," Frush answered. "We're part of the National Security Agency. We're not going for treasure. We're looking for an enemy submarine that's lying at the bottom. I wanted to tell you before. . . ."

"But you didn't," Dave snapped.

"Sorry, it was *top secret*. I had my orders from Washington. I was only to tell any 'outside' help we use once we got to the diving site.

"We're going for the ZRG-89," Frush went on. "It's their latest model. A nuclear sub filled with electronic gear and the newest weapons. And our CIA people tell me that it went down with their code books. We want all of it, Dave."

Dave glared at Frush. "And you want me to go down there and bring it up?"

"Exactly. You *and* I are going to free the ZRG-89 from the underwater canyon. We'll blast the right wall first, then use the underwater tractor to clear the sand and rocks."

"And the owners are just going to sit on their hands and let us walk right in?" Dave snapped.

Frush shook his head. "No. They'll fight us for every inch of sand. They want what's in the sub as much as we do—*more* than we do. In fact, one of their ships is steaming this way and should be here soon."

"Here?" Dave said, surprised.

"Yes, we're here. We're sitting right on top of that beauty. We have no time to lose. And to make matters worse, our radar shows that a severe storm is headed toward us." He turned to the deck officer. "All engines stopped. Lower the anchors. Prepare the sub for launching." The captain turned to Dave. "Ready. Or do I do this alone? And lock you in the brig until this is over?"

Dave sat beside Captain Frush as the minisub eased down into the ocean. "Down fifty . . . seventy . . . one hundred," Frush called out. Dave watched the depth gauge. "Nine hundred . . . nine-fifty . . ."

Frush stopped the descent and guided the sub through the underwater canyon. As they moved around a bend, the port light focused on a large metal object.

"It's the ZRG-89," Dave said nervously.

Frush clicked on his microphone.

"Frush to *Explorer*. Have located 'Red One.' Prepare all hands for salvage. We'll start with the sub's bow." He took off his headset. "All right, Dave, let's get to work."

They dressed in the special underwater pressure suits. They attached small breathing tanks to their backs, then stepped into the minisub's release chamber. The compartment filled with water. Frush opened a hatch and they swam out into the canyon. Dave's light flashed on one side of the submarine. Frush followed him on an underwater sled that was packed with equipment.

Dave reached the side of the ZRG-89. His light traced the outline of the ship. "We're in luck," he told Frush over a small radio built into the helmet. "I can get into the sub through the main hatch."

"Okay," Frush replied. He guided the sled to the bottom. He was about to hand Dave a welding kit when suddenly a gray shark lunged at him. Frush screamed as the shark's teeth pierced his diving suit.

Dave fumbled for his harpoon gun, found it and fired two barbs at the shark. The first missed, but the second plunged into its side. Dave put his arm around Captain Frush and swam wildly back toward the minisub. Frush's diving suit was torn. And it was losing pressure.

Dave swam with all his strength. In another 30 seconds the suit would collapse, and the pressure would crush the captain.

Dave reached the release compartment

and pulled Frush into the small chamber. He bolted it tightly, allowed the pressure to adjust, and reentered the minisub. The captain's shoulder was torn and bleeding. Dave packed it with gauze and stopped the flow of blood.

"Thanks," Frush said weakly.

"That was too close for comfort," Dave said. He picked up the microphone. "We're going up. I'll alert the ship."

"Not yet," Frush insisted. "You have to get into that sub. You've got to get their manuals and the code books."

The radio crackled. "*Explorer* to Frush. Ship is approaching. Distance is five miles. Do you read me? The ship is moving in fast."

"Now you have to work fast," Frush

said firmly. "Get into the sub, take what you can and *get out.*"

Dave strapped a small speargun and a packet of five steel-tipped darts to his right leg. Then he entered the release chamber and went into the water again. He swam back to the Soviet sub. The sled with the welding equipment was on its side, but the tanks and torches weren't damaged. He set up the gear near the main hatch and began to cut away the layers of steel. The work was difficult. The cutting torch barely etched a line in the sub's outer plates.

It's no use, Dave thought, and he stopped. *Maybe I can find the emergency compartment and enter through there.* His light inched over the smooth side of the vessel as he searched for an entry. Then he found it: a small, man-sized hatch near the bow of the sub. As he began to turn the lock wheel, five dots of light, about a hundred yards away, appeared and moved closer. *Frogmen,* Dave mutterd to himself. He worked more quickly. He got the hatch open, and was inside the ZRG-89.

It was a strange feeling being inside the sub. The power was on and the lights flickered as Dave moved around cautiously. As he went through the sub he took pictures with a minicamera. First the chart area, then the main deck.

A loud clang sent a chill down his spine.

The frogmen had reached the sub. They clamped themselves onto the sides and were searching the area. Dave hurried toward the communications center. He had to find the sub's code books. He pulled open a metal door leading to the center of the ship. An explosion sent him flying backwards. The crew had set booby traps before they abandoned the sub.

Dave's face was cut and his body felt numb. He pulled himself up, staggered forward, and moved into the next area.

Suddenly there was another series of noises from the sub's hull. The frogmen were combing the outside of the ship. There wasn't time to search the cabin for the top-secret code book. Dave crammed a book that looked like a manual into a pocket of his wet suit and hurried back to the emergency hatch. A searchlight beamed into his face as he entered the water. Another focused to the left. The shaft of a sea spear whizzed past his head.

Dave moved quickly back toward the minisub as the frogmen came after him. As he entered the small compartment, an explosion tore through the water. The minisub rolled and turned. Dave and the captain were thrown from side to side. Another blast. The water pushed the sub wildly about on the bottom of the ocean. Then it was calm.

Dave lay on the floor of the sub for a few minutes. When he was finally able to look out the window, all he saw was deep water. No frogmen. No submarine. *Those explosions must have come from the other sub*, he thought. *When it blew, it took the men with it.*

Dave dragged himself toward Frush. He was alive, but badly cut about the head. "Hang in there, Captain," Dave groaned. He inched toward the radio. "Colvin to *Explorer*. Colvin to *Explorer*. Do you read me?" There was silence. *Maybe the explosions blew our circuits*, he thought.

Dave pulled himself to a sitting position. His arms ached and his legs were bruised. He steadied himself at the sub's controls and began to raise the small craft off the bottom. Nine hundred . . . eight . . . six-twenty . . . Finally it broke the surface.

Waves 30 feet high swept over the sub. A driving rain and a 90-mile-per-hour wind pushed the craft onto its side. Dave had surfaced in a typhoon. He fought to get control of the sub. When he did he took it below to calmer waters. He would ride out the storm in relative safety deep beneath the surface.

The next day Dave brought the minisub to the surface. The sea was calm and the sky a bright blue. Sunlight sparkled on the water.

"I guess we made it," he said as he helped Captain Frush to the deck.

Frush smiled. "Thanks for saving my life." He touched the bandages wrapped tightly about his head.

"The typhoon must have pushed the

Global Explorer off course," Dave remarked. "Well, it can't be too far from here. We should be able to make contact and link up sometime today."

Frush nodded. "There's a lot to do when we get back. All those pictures will help our intelligence people. And that book? It's not their top-secret code, but it still looks very useful."

Dave watched as some dolphins leaped out of the water and then plunged back down. As he inhaled the crisp air, he thought about his narrow escape at the bottom of the ocean. It was good to be alive. He was feeling lucky again.